# FLOWERS & SKY

## BOOKS BY AARON SHURIN

*The Skin of Meaning: Collected Literary Essays and Talks*

*Citizen*

*King of Shadows*

*Involuntary Lyrics*

*A Door*

*The Paradise of Forms: Selected Poems*

*Unbound: A Book of AIDS*

*Into Distances*

*A's Dream*

*The Graces*

*Giving up the Ghost*

*The Night Sun*

# FLOWERS & SKY

*Two Talks*

AARON SHURIN

entre ríos books

Entre Ríos Books
www.entreriosbooks.com
Seattle, Washington

FLOWERS & SKY: TWO TALKS

ISBN: 978-0-9973957-2-3 (paper)

*Cover image: Almond Blossom, 1890 (oil on canvas)*
*Van Gogh, Vincent (1853–90) / Van Gogh Museum, Amsterdam,*
*The Netherlands / Bridgeman Images*

First Edition. ERB 004.
Printed in the United States.

# TABLE OF CONTENTS

Preface  *vii*

___ONE___

SOMETIME OF THE NIGHT

*11*

___TWO___

THE SKY FOR EXAMPLE

*31*

___THREE___

SIX SKY POEMS

*41*

___APPENDIX___

THE SKY IN *CITIZEN*

*51*

Notes  *59*

Acknowledgements  *62*

Audio  *63*

# PREFACE

The figures of powers governing the imagination write
themselves in skies and flowers.

Or so it seems. These essays were written and delivered
as talks on two separate occasions in the spring and fall of
2016. Though the events were distinct, my methods were
similar: for each piece a governing image channeled me
back into my own work in a kind of recursive voyage of
discovery. *Flowers and Sky*: I seem to have been commanded
by these figures across a lifetime of writing, and so I took
the opportunity to try to unravel their arrivals — to mark
my developing interests and abilities but also pay homage
to their power as a constant resource, their inexhaustible
resonance in the shimmer of my own reverberations. By
the end I'd pursued a set of congruencies as if performing
an autobiography in parts, in attendance to the powers I
harnessed that made a life in me. I vetted my writing in

the service of a deep romance of images, to lose myself again in a discipline of flowers under a paradise of skies...

To enter the flower or parse the sky required a certain general focus for sure, but the very form and structure of a talk suggested personal presence. I wrote in the first person to *be* the person, and raised citations from my own work to illustrate the image-adventure charging my work. The actual occasion of the talks, of course, included a live audience: I hope you can listen to the recording we made and hear the *live* in it, so that the silences of time and distance might dissolve in the timbre of my voice. The piece is the complete "Sometime of the Night," a set of meditations circling around the famous "flower soliloquy" from *A Midsummer Night's Dream*, from which sonorities abound. The spell is in the petal, so to speak, so lean back... and let the wild vowels bloom!

April and October, Alabama and Washington state: There were great globs of magnolias working the high branches, and shifting streaks of gray and white pelting the big pine ridge. The first talk was given as part of "The Poet's Shakespeare," for the University of Alabama / Tuscaloosa's Strode Shakespeare symposium. The second was delivered on a panel called "What is poetics?" as part of the University of Washington / Bothell's Fall Convergence in Poetry.

Much gratitude to the conference organizers and fellow travelers alike, who privileged questions over answers to make an art of listening... and whose generous attention helped amplify these talks into conversations.

*"a breeze of words teasing out the substance of the sky..."*

# ONE

# SOMETIME OF THE NIGHT

*"The Poet's Shakespeare"*
THE HUDSON STRODE PROGRAM IN RENAISSANCE STUDIES
UNIVERSITY OF ALABAMA, TUSCALOOSA
April 2016

## SOMETIME OF THE NIGHT

I keep circling back, as if trying to unwind a spell... as if I could un-pop the rhymes, unthread the music, and release the measure... But no, not to unmake them: to come again to their making, to feel anew the sway of the spell and the bell of the rhyme and the swell of the measure — four hundred years strong in themselves, and fifty years alive in my own body. So I return again and again to my dream, my *Midsummer Night's Dream*, as — what now? — Puck with a gray beard? A goat-boy with a cane? — and to the lines that seem to have been my birthright: Oberon's flower soliloquy, spoken to Puck as a prelude to delivering to or on Titania the magic flower-juice that will awaken her to her fate, to the intoxication of love, to falling instantly and transformingly in love — just as the spoken lines awakened me to my own fate — of falling in love with language through the transforming power of poetry.

"I know a bank…" Shakespeare's King of Fairies tells Puck, Act II, Scene i, in the enchanted woods near Athens,

I know a bank where the wild thyme blows,
Where oxlips and the nodding violet grows,
Quite overcanopied with luscious woodbine,
With sweet musk roses and with eglantine:
There sleeps Titania sometime of the night,
Lulled in these flowers with dances and delight;
And there the snake throws her enamelled skin,
Weed wide enough to wrap a fairy in…

Yes — as I have often told the tale — at the age of seventeen I thought to play Oberon in our high school production of *Dream*, and buried my face full force in those flowers, inhaled them, absorbed them, and declaimed the lines in rooms, on city streets, in my bed and in my sleep I suppose — and *still* declaim them — though it was the role of Puck that was given to me, it was Puck who claimed me, and Puck who I became. And yet, myself transformed by what I'd memorized, a Puck who owned the ritual and the rite to command *himself* to service — to spell himself, I'll say, to awaken himself into love and to figure the love in language in the shape of poems… "I know a bank," I say, and around me the flowers bloom, the flower-words in their spectral aura and rich sensory evocation — incantatory zeal!

And what of this bouquet of text, this enchanted embankment where fairies sleep and wake? What of the sounds that melt the mind, of the scents that flavor the spell, of the petals that form the matrix of meanings that power the poem...? Of the woozy beauty, the lassitude, the sleeping figure of the dream, the wildness, the lusciousness and sweetness, the musk, the lips, the bed of skin, the night, the night, the night; what of the violet hue, the rosebud and the egg, the light and shine, the mad growth of things, and the knowing... and the knowing...

Eight short lines... But pull apart the petals (gently! gently!) of this spray of primal energy, a hypnotic syllabary spreading outwards in its hush of woozy beauty, pull apart the petals to show the links: for the lassitude [*lulled in these flowers*], for the sleeping figure of the dream [*there sleeps Titania*], the wildness [*where the wild thyme blows*], the lusciousness and sweetness and the musk [*with luscious woodbine, with sweet musk roses*], the lips [*where oxlips*], the bed of skin [*the snake throws her enamelled skin*], the night [*there sleeps Titania sometime of the night*], the violet hue [*and the nodding violet grows*], the rosebud and the egg [*with sweet musk roses and with eglantine*], the light and shine [*delight... enamelled skin*], the mad growth of things [*the nodding violet grows, quite overcanopied*], and of course, the knowing, the deep knowing [*I know a bank*]...

So I fell (and fall) under Shakespeare's spell. I felt the sonorities; I swooned at what Pound (according to Robert Duncan) called "the tone leading of vowels" — that unfolding rise and fall and shape-shift of transitions in the vocal pattern — and the circulations of the rhymes, the tickle of alliteration and the arousal of assonance, the full phonemic play in speech (these words are *spoken*) that seemed to register in sounds the total sensory field of flower, person, wind, ground, and sleep. As though the soliloquy itself were a waking dream into which one fell into full *seeming*.

What did oxlips or eglantine look like, what were their attributes of color or scent? For many many years I didn't know or care: The flowers were their names, and they bloomed as sonic text, not visual image. They were bursting nodes in a sound pattern, auditory evocations in the service of an elaborate music of transformations, by which the players — the readers and the spectators — might come to participate in the enchantments of love.

Now I can see the yellow and pink blossoms, and gather the scents from what I know, and feel the stems and foliage appropriate to a riparian grove — of course Shakespeare knew what flowers would thrive on his bank, and might emit the fumes to cloud the senses for his dream. And from this Renaissance model I quickly came to understand that the "language of flowers" — the taxonomy and identification, the knowledge of their attributes, the ability to name their names, was part of a poet's duty. As in most things poetic, the goal was to *pay attention*. To see the world in its constituent parts — and only by raising the parts in their specificity could one begin to engage the living whole. If I wanted to be a real poet — and very soon I did — I would have to know my flowers.

I did have some inclination and some preparation. As a boy at summer camp I reveled in the Eastern fields of black-eyed Susans — knew them and sought them out and marveled at them, with their black berry-lumps at the center, and long buttery fringes. And in the canoes on those woodland ponds I slipped through water lilies opening and closing like hands, overjoyed at their pastel hardiness, their drunken starbursts of pink and cream. Later in Texas, with my first-ever backyard (I was nine), I planted borders of riotous zinnias, those crenellated macaroons in moony hues, and reached a pure satisfaction in junior stalks of morning glories, twining and trumpeting their iridescent blue.

Those were gentle forays, and not yet connected to a poet's craft. But in the summer of 1969, having formed, from the classroom on out, a deep apprenticeship and growing friendship with Denise Levertov, the great American poet, I found myself walking through the Maine woods and fields with her, as she pointed out clusters of forget-me-nots, and raspberries ripe for picking, and we stood gaping before a great poplar, thrilled by the wind — "that poplar," she writes in "Writing to Aaron" from *Life in the Forest*, "that gave us its open secret, pressed on us all we could grasp, and more, / of vibrating, silvergreen being." *Pay attention*. A few days earlier I'd read her poem "Annuals", whose flower names — cosmos and the Marvel of Peru — rivaled those of Shakespeare's in their evocative power. *Attending* these plantings for her garden, from cotyledon on, she watches in worried suspense as no flower buds appear: "If August passes / flowerless, / and the frosts come," she asks, "will I have learned to rejoice enough / in the sober wonder of / green healthy leaves?" So I learned to watch in wonder, and find the names for what I saw, and peel back the names to discover the sensory details of color or scent, or meet head-on the richness of the no-flower flower.

I had begun my first journal in 1968, a thin tightly lined "Record" with a black pebbled cover, and it bore witness to my awakening interest in poetry, as I transcribed "Annuals," and, soon after, Sylvia Plath's "Poppies in July," ("Little poppies, little hell flames"). The summer after my visit with Denise, I traveled to Europe, and the journal finds me walking through the miniature hills and dales of Wales. On July 30, 1970, I looked across to the horizon where hilltops mounted the far distances, only to discover them at my feet a short while later. Fooled by the scale of the terrain, what I'd presumed to be mountains far away turned out to be little hills a few hundred yards in front of me. "A land of fairy-tales and little people," I wrote; "towns nestled right into the crook of a hill, invisible from a mile away." And then this first journal of my writing apprenticeship comes to a close with a single phrase: "Along a little riverbank, patches of forget-me-nots." And pressed onto the final page with a fading piece of tape is a small still-unforgettable spray of once-blue flowers.

If flowers by their nature have a look-at-me quality — their goal after all is to get noticed and pollinated — I rose to the task with the fervor of a dizzy bee on the make. *Toot Suite* of 1978 charges into the fray, with a final poem of the rain-drenched sequence rhapsodizing:

> the wet rose     up the randy roots, a fibrous pull
> of ooze blooming, the tumescent reach, ground
> hiving, heaving, leafing, the flung seed bursting
> the rising rose

For sure I was feeling my way through a host of formal adventures in *Toot Suite*, but what's already clear is that flowers and I would meet in a zone of unabashed exuberance. By 1997's prose meditation "July," from *Unbound: A Book of AIDS*, I'd flung myself shamelessly towards a table-top bowl of almost-mythic roses, summer forever: "these swollen roses puffed on the dining room table, creaming pale magenta, lavender and pink in a moiré pattern, fading color into color the way silk does, seizing light and inhabiting the shine from within."

If I pushed on the noble powers of description to exercise my flamboyant sympathy, I was still learning boundaries, still testing my gardener's pen. *Involuntary Lyrics*, from 2005, rides its nervy syntax into a more compressed encounter, as I walk among "moon-pod wild thistles, shaggy, noon / seeming midnight in their spooky glare" and "wind-silvery eucalyptus leaves and their pentagram nuts." Or I sit on a log in a park where "heart- / shaped clover fluffs up, dew drops play globe, stinky acacia's blooming youth- / like glandular smell befits / a day seems young..." with "plum blossoms pinking the air." Or I address the sober but lovely blooming bush of *leptospermum*: "Dear *leptospermum*, tiny magenta flowers on needly branches, please know / I meant no offense / mistakenly conflating you with AIDS-related intestinal disorder *cryptosporidium*." Or, returning to a summer song, "Air's stilled again as incipient summer does, suppressed / breathing pulls truth / out of poppies blaring just / the yellow condensation pure sun lies / in," with "hawk on cypress branch squawking at me /by best /perchable fallen long, scotch broom yellow too, perfuming the still air as time itself be / speaking tongue..." Thistles at midnight, pentagram pods, dewdrops that appear to be whole globes, the mysterious *leptospermum*, hushed breathing as poppies extrude sunlight... You begin to sense the possibility of an enchanted embankment forming.

For a poet the language of flowers engages the world in its radiant particularities, reenacts an active seduction of sight and scent, reveals the primal power of fruition in cyclical time, and carries the charges of symbolic orders from folklore to science. "*Pay attention*," I tell myself. "Learn the names, study the attributes, look, inhale, attempt the impossible: *represent!*" In *King of Shadows* from 2008, the lyric essay gives me full measure to spread my... err... petals. In an essay called "Dahlias," about the futility of metaphor and description, I stand before Golden Gate Park's dahlia garden "in preposterous full bloom" and nevertheless give it a rousing try:

> About fifty square yards of outsized, overpetaled, shaggy booming flowers, speckled and striped, ruffled and layered, and speaking colors I've never even known the name of, much less how to evoke. Magenta and mauve? Too Victorian, and too stable. Bright yellow? Too singular, and lacking a thrust

of energy. Red? But with black bleeding it. Orange:
You must be kidding — this livid, churning, moonlit
fire?

The range of dahlia shapes here taxes taxonomy.
Some have fluted petals, like rows of curled tongues,
that amass in starched collars and speak Dutch.
Some have the blowzy overdetermination of kings
and queens, mighty, almost-weary figureheads
overhanging their propping stalks, those plebeian
supporters. They seem to defy the appropriate laws
of architecture and physics that gather around plant
physiology (physiognomy?), too big, too weighty,
too fraught with glamour and purposelessness.

What is a flower but a momentary eruption of
streaming energy, of the power of generation and the
condensation of senses into a fleeting burst of creative
impulse, a poem blasting forth in temporal vibrations by
which we might fall in love with the world again as though
awakening from a dream. If Oberon's soliloquy had dazzled
me into a kind of mnemonic stupor — though an ecstatic
stupor for sure — in the end the heart of the matter was
transactional: the interrelated responses of gardener and
garden, of the perfume and the inhaler, the player and the
audience, of the spell-caster and the spellbound, constitute
a mutual magnetic twining like a double helix as an avenue

to the pure flowing life-force. Shakespeare's flower-strewn bank is, after all, purposefully interactive, abloom in the service of transformative magic that will be visited upon Titania and the Athenian lovers. If some blossoms lull us into a dream-state, defenses down, power off, they merely set the stage for another flower that will juice our juices and turn us on... *way* on.

In 2003 I sublet a house in ultra-verdant Marin County, for a small sum and a promise to tend to the stunning garden in back. What was proposed as a small watering chore turned out to be a herculean effort of weeding, soaking, and mothering. In "Reciprocity" I detail the struggle and the reward, as the garden responds to my care with an explosion of feeling (and an explosion of descriptive language fueled by a 150-word sentence):

New perennials constantly sprang up unannounced, filling-in small barren spots with their surprise attractions: tiny yellow-chinned violets, effulgent purple dahlias, a two-headed pink gerbera daisy, willful strands of magenta sweet peas that would climb your hand if you left it resting too long, one pure but incongruous fumy gardenia — while over the course of the summer the stalwart artichoke opened its crustacean leaves into a livid, heaving crown of scintillating blue, enrapturing the bees who grazed *inside* the oversized bloom as if it were a meadow; the strawberries dropped their hot, sweet hearts into my hands by the cupful; and the morning glories, who *owned* the house, raged over the front wall, withered in a morning minute, and bled their indigo trumpets into translucent pink disks, shedding them finally like wrinkled carapaces onto the porch steps — then blared moonily again the next day, blue-bright as high twilight and uncountable in their fluorescent profusion. Oregano and marjoram blossomed and began to dry in the air, spiking the night with hot summer undertones.

I think I could say I reached saturation. The reciprocity was truly engaged. After sleeping, waking, and falling in love, the marriage of gardener and plant is the garden, as the marriage of the poet and the language of flowers is the poem, and the union of Renaissance writer and postmodern scribe an intertextual trans-epochal dance across time in the form of a florid address. Then let me be Oberon who casts the spell, and Puck who carries the potion, and Titania who falls madly in love — all together, all at once.

Oberon: She shall pursue it with the soul of love.

Puck:     I'll put a girdle round about the earth in
          forty minutes.

Titania:  What angel wakes me from my flowery bed?

In fact my compositional dance with Shakespeare and
*Midsummer* has revolved around more than flowers. In the
title piece of *King of Shadows*, I tell the full and surrounding
tale of my performance of Puck, and splice small phrases
from the play into a narrative of diving in and coming out:
*in* to the poetic music of the play and *out* to the arms of
men. For the play served me as a dual initiation into the
two great body-and-soul arcs of my life.

The memorization and performance of Shakespeare's
language set my whole spirit thrumming like a tuning
fork. For "when one performs in a play one experiences
in the body's echo chamber the language of all the roles.
In verse, the brain's muscle memory sets the encased skel-
eton vibrating, an experience that can only be described
as holistic." The excitement and nuanced tension of the
high-wire act by which the play's language, exemplified
by the flower sequence, enacted poetry's dynamic drama
of sound versus sense, awakened my imagination to the
level of art:

Poetry is that literary form in which both the depth function and the surfaces of language are activated, and, pleasures abounding, you are constantly threatened with being in one at the expense of the other. There is no rest. To be in a poem is to live in that constant peril by which meaning is transferred in and out of its form, language performing sensual, decorative, counter-semantic moves just as it absorbs them into structures of content. "Luscious woodbine," and "sweet musk roses" would break away from the very bank in which they're planted, as the reader, "lulled in these flowers", loses his "odoriferous" way... The vow of poets attends such elegant suspension as sport, <u>where we are spirits of another sort</u>.

From the moment I'd announced, "I know a bank..." I'd taken that lifetime vow.

As for the other vibrations, accepting this role, saying "Yes" to donning ballet slippers and tights, and twerking around the stage all atwinkle, while at the same time feeling the satyrish undertow of cloven hooves, ignited the simmering flame in me that burned through my late-adolescent nights:

The boy there turned in his bed, restless, a King of Fairies but surrounded by the shadows of men, boys, men, their shadowy parts, turning in his bed, whispering, "Hey... Boy... it can be done; <u>pursue it with the soul of love</u>"; shadowy parts rubbing him <u>through the glimmering night</u>.

And because of that, a few short weeks after the production, "I met a man in a Boston dormitory who twinkled at me ceremoniously and invited me to his room. His hair curled tight like a satyr and his eyes were <u>nodding violets</u>." Having been awakened and initiated by *A Midsummer Night's Dream*, I did, in fact, with little hesitation, say "Yes" again. Then:

He slid me a long, mischievous smile and stretched out his arms. "<u>Take hands with me</u>," he prompted tenderly...

*"<u>and rock the ground whereon these sleepers be</u>."*

And I did.

The circle circles but doesn't close. In 1985 Barron's began a series of study guides, "Book Notes," and I was invited to participate. There on the list up for grabs was *A Midsummer Night's Dream*, and so, twenty years after my performance, I returned to the play as a scholar, and within the rubric of the series lent my enthusiasms to high school students everywhere looking for an end-run around Shakes. There, in a note on "Titania's resting place," I list again the famous flowers and suggest, "to help feel the magic of this passage, you might say these words out loud" since they "roll across the tongue with what seems to be a magical power." If somewhere along cold institutional corridors, a soccer jock or science nerd or band member is mouthing the words "luscious woodbine" and "sweet musk roses" I will consider my job well done.

And still there are the orange lilies.

Let me tell you about the orange lilies.

"As morning settled she watched the petal of the overblown lily — orange cream — fall like a fledgling," the poem "Uncontainable" from 2012's *Citizen* begins, as this unnamed woman enters a zone of almost psyche-delic observation. The overblown (overcanopied?) flowers become a portal to another dimension — or at least their transformations of color and line so absorb her attention that her own containing lines and colors begin to dissolve and transform through a kind of "amoebic assonance." She is rhyming with the lilies. In this interchange of "vamping materium" — the curled-back lilies in morning light — the poem lets loose its own restraints on language and — all caution to the wind — enacts a textual symbiosis of person and plant in a gymnastic transference of form, "as though she'd bridled at tedious common sense and in a spew let fly her own... curling jet... her backflip aurora... her upward peeling splash, sprung lunge *scintille*..." In a lexical swoon of music daring sense — and with full power of an exclamation point — the transubstantiation reaches climax as "apricot eucharist spillover *jeté*!"

Perhaps I'll imagine that students somewhere, walking faceless hallways, will repeat these words in a befuddled thrill, and feel their arching bodies blossom and blow. I know I've never written a string of words as extravagant as *apricot eucharist spillover jeté!* And I'm not quite sure anyone else would *let* themselves. But behind them lie decades of practice and rehearsal — of tree and leaf and bud and vine and bloom. They are my "sweet musk roses," and in their swoon my spell found its making.

So let me be Oberon who casts the spell, and Puck who carries the potion, and Titania who falls madly in love — but let me be, too, the magic flower itself, swollen by Cupid's arrow and pulsing with the juice of pure passion — a wildflower *in excelsis* — held aloft in moonlight and squeezed upon... well... *your* eyes!

# TWO

# THE SKY FOR EXAMPLE

*"What is poetics?"*

FALL CONVERGENCE: FORM AND FOUNDATION

UNIVERSITY OF WASHINGTON, BOTHELL

October 2016

# THE SKY FOR EXAMPLE

About thirty-five years ago a reader embarrassed me by noting how frequently the word "sky" appeared in my poems — or was it in just one book? The number was alarming, as I remember, and I was chagrined by the possibility of my sloppy oversight, or, conversely, of my now-naked linguistic obsession. Some two decades later, another scrutinizing reader pointed out my intemperate usage of "mouth" and "lips." That, at least, was a fixation I could understand, a kind of gay marriage between homo-carnality and poetic sonority, avatars both of the oral. But the sky? I'd admitted to many delicious compulsions and inhabited many voices and masks, but I hadn't yet said, "I'm a Sky Queen."

Which is not the same as being Queen of the Sky. I'm not particularly partial to sky deities — especially in their patriarchal incarnations — Zeus, Yahweh — though the matriarchal versions are more to my temperament. In fact, the frontispiece to my first book, *The Night Sun*, (its cover has an indigo night sky) has a detail from a Greek vase, c. 450 BC, showing two dancing figures. A young man, suspended in vase-space, salutes his larger partner. She is seriously twirling in a voluminous hoop skirt, whose ballooning sphere recalls a planet in rotation. A chandelier headdress of concentric circles, alive with lit candles, crowns her head and signals her power: She is all orbit and axis as she spins the flaming galaxy that is her other face and form. I am partial to *her* kind of sky god. The title poem of *The Night Sun* opens melodramatically with "*The sky was blood /shot*," and closes just a bit less so with "*Heavenly fingers /that punch holes in the nightsky /and call them stars...*" [November, 1976]

OK, I thought, post critic, so I'm attracted to the sky. In the Getty museum in Malibu I saw a tiny archaic figure, Anatolian, c. 2500 BC, whose head was set on his neck with a permanent upward tilt. The printed label said "stargazer." Later, on the far-seeing hilltop ruins of Monte Albán near Oaxaca, a telescopic perch wide as the horizon, I purchased a similar tiny stone man, this time Zapotec, whose head was also angled up — way up — slung back so far on his neck that his face was almost parallel to the sky. "See," the carver showed me, "he's an astronomer." I too raise my chin, but I'm a poet so I reach for my pen. At the very top of my notebook page, as if it were floating in air, I write "Sky-Watcher."

After *The Night Sun*, you can follow the sky as it hovers over each book in sequence, from "*The moon is a puppy in the sun's sky*" in 1980's *Giving up the Ghost* right through to "*How do you thread a sigh so it attaches to the sky and rises like a mind on fire*," from 2012's *Citizen* (with eighteen instances of sky; see appendix). There are *lures*; you have lures; writers have *lures*. You return again and again because the charm holds, the magic commands, the glow reveals and reveals... Some figures will not be emptied (be it H.D.'s rose or Creeley's line) but maintain and sustain the work; the lure is the paramour of the work. Somewhere along the way I wrote, happily, "*The sky: the sea with wings.*" At some point I almost sang, "*For a person mirrored in the sea the sky is melodic.*" And once, dutifully, devotedly, I met the immensity as "*The sky covered the sky.*"

For sure it is a cipher for the blank page up there, and as such invites inscription — thus my continuing attempts at entering its overarching domain, at invoking through metaphor or measure the immeasurable. A notebook empyrean. (Leslie Scalapino wrote a piece about my work and called it "The Sky of Text.") Is there any bigger canvas available? Anything so present but so empty?

Whose porousness invites attempts to shape and mold it, to embrace it or mount it, to fly in it or float in it or ride it to the end, "*up into the pogo sky with arms akimbo*"? It is omnipresent yet utterly local. It is grandiosely public, but it courts the personal by reflection: the rhymes it shares with "I" and "my" and "eye," and the mirrored glint it shines in someone's eyes:

> *His* light, his *light*, from off his face — or was it *in* his face? Like that shiny planet of the mind that is *in* my sky. He's my sky for today. *His* light, his *light*, which is *my* light in my mind... Is he *in* my face, are my eyes his sky?

I'm not unilaterally *for* "sky"— Shelley's unpronounceable "skiey speed" is one of the clumsiest phrases in English poetry (though I haven't forgotten it), which is odd since Shelley seems to *live* in the sky, swirling in a spirit-body just this side of incarnation. But for corrective there is Robert Duncan's beautifully plaintive: "But it was for a clearing of the sky, for a blue radiance, my thought cried." And there is William Carlos Williams, who doesn't say the word but reverentially brings it into presence —

> Above
> among the shufflings

             of the distant
             cloud-rifts
             vaporously
             the unmoving
             blue


I wrote a dance for a friend, who wanted to mark his survival with HIV. In the central movement he slowly, determinedly, walks through the city and keeps walking, as "sky panels" mark his steadfast pursuit. "*Sky panels move and shift,*" it begins:

> Things move *through* them and *in* them. Clouds, birds, airplanes; the spires of tall buildings. The sky moves *in* me and *through* me. Air currents swirl and bend; my back bends forward in the wind. On the pavement in a gray puddle the sky shimmers bluely, a pinch of white dissolving as the cloud-wisps drift.

Recently I've laid the charge against myself that writing about the sky is writing *in lieu of…* That I want to write about race and gender, brutality, violence, infamy, and tyranny, but every time I open my notebook (I've complained) I seem to just want to write about the sky. So it's useful to remember that in my dance about AIDS the sky held its power as a righteous force, a vision of sustenance against the collapse of governmental intervention, against physical breakdown and civic antipathy and aggression. It held as a vision of endurance and light. And, as it turns out, I did write the more historically charged poem that I said I couldn't — and the sky was there anyway: in the middle of San Francisco's seeming descent into social dispossession and greed I mourned its loss! *"Once I was a sailor when the sky was one thing, a blue breath from pole to pole I caught in my wild hair and out-flung hands..."* As if, now, no wild hair, no sky...

Image, fact, symbol, vision, element, epithet, aura ... And still there is the question of blue and its vagrant hues — translucent and transient, ever-transforming. How many blues for the sky... but what is *sky-blue*? The color of height, the color of depth, the color of vastness and the color of distance, the color of cosmos, the color of space, the color of the future and the color of horizon, the color of the ether and the color of heaven...

Sky-blue condenses the atmosphere and gives it substance, a tonal materiality that puts a ceiling on the illimitable nothingness of space, and lets us feel properly planetary: earth rooted, earth bound. Sky-blue is our canopy and roof; it covers and shields us from endless amplitude — the first panel in the structure of home.

Look up: It's a template for projection and hallucination, a field for omens to inscribe their verdicts in birds. Look up: It's a backdrop for an endless shifting narration: those dinosaurs and palaces, sailing ships and minarets of clouds. [*"Look at the sky: it reeks of projection. Look at my eyes: they're tools of the sky."*]

I lie on my back on a bench as though it were an analyst's couch, and let my brain go Rorschach on the sky: Size favors epic battles, pleasure domes, lovers' faces in cinematic fades... But it's the transitions themselves that move me most, a kaleidoscope of shifting shapes whose joyous, restless, startling foment enacts a poet's dream: the constant regeneration of figures in the language of clouds.

And behind, there is serenity, and framework, and wonder. And above, there is plenitude, and totality, and openness. Is it the gateway to our feel for the eternal, our ever-present sense that things go on and through, our tinted picture of the farthest reaches by which we might keep ourselves in scale? Its attraction is its comprehensive volume, its map with no borders, its spatial inevitability, its absorbent generosity, and its purchase on the inviolable direction of "up." Of course there are dark and lowering skies, but my sky is bright. It has hope in it, so it serves the open text. No limits,

*"and edge to edge the blue absolute..."*

## CODA

What is poetics?

You turn it in your hand like a snow globe, and shake it to see its full effects. What do you write, how do you write, what do you mean, what do you frame and what do you follow? What have you made and what have you found? What do you honor, what do you savor, what do you need to encounter...?

The sky for example.

## THREE

## SIX SKY POEMS

IN THE MIST

On Monday the window was open; the night followed me
and couldn't be quieted. I smoked at the sky, lay down in
the rain — blind devotion — for a person mirrored in the
sea the sky is melodic.

He was a man — (fear the awakening) — a woman — (my
lovers passed in illusion) — I rode in a forest — (religious
instinct?) — opened the exaggerated sun — a kind of
sweating lassitude.

I lie on my couch — everything has changed — patience
of the mists — pump into the entrails of things — he
sucks up sunlight, pounding with joy, precise as a cello.
Someone comes along and separates me from the form.
Evangelical milk and humanitarian thighs and socialist
drapery: It's not enough to have wings; when I unfold them
your perfume rises from the paper.

Great stretches of water — a gray vapor that appears to be
moving — sunset melted dark ink — mass of trees — my
ministerial partition — with the space of days before an
address. As dancers ripple and retreat their faces remain
movements of a body.

I thought of her dance without meaning, whistling through the bushes. My feet ahead of me — one among others — trembling resources — between that enormity and the moon on the hilltop here. Now I can hear part of myself penetrated by individualities. The city is immense.

This changeable sky sees the buildings differently. There are more flowers in the house than in the ground. The floor a forest of dark olive trees, sea at the far end...

Shadows glide beyond the plains with white sails — almost in the air — moving noiselessly over the surface of things. Another ocean climbed the mist, adjusting that human anatomy: horizon lines. I forget what I stayed at home to do. The blue spread out.

With my elbows on the table I'm going back to that place.

## THE PLACE

One will take a model for them and become plastically concrete. The conversation see the words when they want to. Those walks or this figure will come out of most things, but that doesn't mean it's natural. There's a head — how beautiful it is! — if I may call it so. As for me who has eyes it's doubly stimulating, because I'm sitting here in silence — and then to swallow oneself as one is in order to sit down and rest...!

A phase of life isn't over then, but one begins more clearly. I feel a power of color, and wonder how it will develop. The clouds of the grass, for instance, when I look at them — that isn't called correctness, or the patches of raining road felt by a person — himself evidently — while now we can talk it over also suffered in the story. Such calculations don't intend emotion or difficulties; everything is simplified in so far as it's not chaos.

When I say I have my everyday life, everyone must decide for himself. If things had happened the mere suggestion of the thing would occupy a certain rank in my own people. A simple word remains a wound and cannot be healed the first day. I hope you understand what battle this was.

So it is here, inside the evening sky, dark as a cave, most realistically. In order to give you an idea of the shape of a leg they stand in the gardens; on many faces they look faded from nearby, very faded. Narrower strips of color imagine the horizon. The sky covered in sky.

That same spot, if one works, becomes light. What I wanted to say is that we could walk here together.

# THE PART UNSEEN

*Is this the something else*, the part unseen, the antidote of clouds, the sculptural path revealed, the winding staircase tucked behind a maple door...? Is there a person crouching in the foreground, among the rocks and reeds, or jumping in the background — up into the pogo sky with arms akimbo or folded like a chair, daring the bourgeois clouds or *of* them? I think he can't decide whether to fly or die... The toreador pants grip his shins — or are those plum trees athwart the Plain of Jars...? Is this his lonesome cataract, the last bushwhack, the foxed and spotted contract, the raison d'être welling up, the parallax...? I think he isn't really there, couldn't see the door, didn't need to cure himself of clouds... Is this an alphabet of blood, or disappearing ink? I saw the river peacock-blue mirror from the slowing train in the blue dusk. I think there was a seagull streaking at the bend. It may have been a person in a boat, hauling up his oar to float the curve...

# SONG

*His* light, his *light*, from off his face — or was it *in* his face?
Like that shiny planet of the mind that is *in* my sky. He's
my sky for today. *His* light, his *light*, which is *my* light in
my mind... Is he *in* my face, are my eyes his sky? He was
near translucent after psychedelics when I saw him, was
it *my* high, am I now translucent...? *His* light, his *light*,
coming *through* me, when I saw him on the corner as the
breeze blew from the sky-within or the sky-without like
the birds sing in the bird-trees... *My* planet that he made
today with his eye- and his skin- and his sky-light... *His*
light, his *light*...!

## HE STOOD

*He stamped his feet and opened the door*, stood on the threshold, turned around. The desert light shrank his eyes, sun slammed his face — he almost lost his breath — blond shiny grasses, ring of distant mountains pinking in the haze, the scorched but somehow fertile earth — he wiped his brow — he couldn't go in, he couldn't move, he couldn't say why — as if he too were a thing dried in sunlight, stopped in his tracks in the heat that fixed him in its gaze — rattlesnake Medusa — where he breathed the stinging dusty winds as though a rock inhaling rock — his proper evolution? — and fed on silence as it flowered and fell — the fierce clarity, the fierce restraint — front door behind him hanging open like a thrown shadow as he blazed in place... a man *inside* the view... the zooming arc... and edge to edge the blue absolute...

## STILL WALKING

Look at the sky: it reeks of projection. Look at my eyes:
they're tools of the sky. Look at my feet: still walking.
"Which way are you walking?" Ask the birds. "What are
you singing?" A walk-along song. "How does it go?" *Bird,
dome, pink, breeze.../ mind-light in the alphabet trees...* And
more like that... Look at my smile: it goes up to the right. Is
that my sly inflection, a mark of selection, the pitch of glory,
the angle of erection? "All that, but rhymier." I watched a
man who bought a bouquet; pleasure made him wiggle
as he walked away. He swished unawares; the peonies
winked and smiled to the right. "What was he singing?"
A wiggling song. "How did it go?" Back and forth. "Ah, the
world's a stage." Look at the page.

# APPENDIX

## THE SKY IN *CITIZEN*

## THE SKY IN *CITIZEN*

Was she raising or lowering ladders inside the staggered light, head down as if in thought but seeing the mounted sky; the peeling, corrugated bark; the coppery cigarette butts and polished plywood table tops and dripping mugs of ale, lit up like sunset gulls bound on the dive...?

Or your face in the searchlight projected, sincere and unembellished: a charismatic stupor that equals the sky...

The stone figure's head permanently tilted up — sky watcher — to make an ongoing guidebook — sky writing — or twirl your hoop skirt with appliquéd stars — sky rhymer — and don't you then see the hard facts disintegrate?

In truth it was the flask of the sky I put to my lips like
a castaway, from the ridge of the patio lookout, palm
fronds clashing, the salmon-stucco belltower with its great
pendulous bell — I wanted to — and the clouds whisked
across in flat sheets, streaming plateau, until suddenly
the hot blue sky flares and the hot thick air falls with its
litany of parrot screech, clanging gate, engine cough — I
wanted to —

The sky is already icy clear, cloudless, fuel for projection.

The sky is not my startled face, my molten hive, my thrash-
ing cape...

I could split the seam of any vector — river, lake or draw —
with coots sputtering from mangrove jumbles, surprised
by my sudden proximity — and the imprint of my oar in
the liquid sky barely visible...

How do you thread a sigh so it attaches to the sky and
rises like a mind on fire?

She squints into the future city, a narrator leaning on a verb (she's standing on the curb) as the mottled sky, fog-swirled, throbs and releases, hectoring the pigeons with alternating flares of black and white...

The sky's a mound of abalone dust...

Invades like the morning chill; sweeps the sky like a falling tail section; cleaves the ground like quake boots, iron cleats...

Once I was a stargazing fool — flint eyes — the machinations of constellations — stunned to be under the sky again looking again with my sensor upraised and the dry earth stomped around me — Karpathos — or my body flattened to a mat by summer heat —

As if the sky itself were always a page, molded by the yielding winds... He compacts himself into a wedge, a cone of muscle by the corner of the corner café, and ponders dark men with light skin, light men with dark skin, skin men in

the thicket of his bed with its catalogue of arched backs
as they dive into the sky of sheets, pulsating envelope...

The sky was not her quarry, her index vault or influx
throne, her ornamental nook or private lair.

# NOTES

## SOMETIME OF THE NIGHT

Denise Levertov: "Writing to Aaron" in *Life in the Forest*, New Directions, 1978, p. 5

Denise Levertov: "Annuals" in *The Sorrow Dance*, New Directions, 1966, p. 39

Sylvia Plath: "Poppies in July" in *Ariel*, Harper & Row, 1965, p. 81

"the wet rose..." in *Toot Suite*, Rose Deeprose Press, 1978

"July," from "Unbound" in *The Skin of Meaning*, University of Michigan Press, 2016, p. 109

*Involuntary Lyrics*, Omnidawn, 2005

"Dahlias" in *King of Shadows*, City Lights Books, 2008, p. 91

"Reciprocity" in *King of Shadows*, p. 17

"King of Shadows" in *King of Shadows*, p. 35

"aka George Loutro," *Barron's Book Notes to A Midsummer Night's Dream*, Barron's Educational Series, 1985

"Uncontainable" in *Citizen*, City Lights Books, 2012, p. 67

"The sky was blood / shot," from "The Night Sun" in *The Night Sun*, Gay Sunshine Press, 1976, p. 51

"The moon is a puppy in the sun's sky," from "Return to Delphi" in *Giving up the Ghost*, Rose Deeprose Press, 1980, p. 63

"How do you thread a sigh so it attaches to the sky and rises like a mind on fire," from "Canto Jondo" in *Citizen*, City Lights Books, 2012, p. 65

"The sky: the sea with wings," from "Into Distances" in *Into Distances*, Sun & Moon Press, 1993, p. 17

"For a person mirrored in the sea the sky is melodic," from "In the Mist" in *Into Distances*, p. 97

"The sky covered the sky," from "The Place" in *Into Distances*, p. 59

Leslie Scalapino: "The Sky of Text" in *The Front Matter, Dead Souls*, Wesleyan University Press, 1996, p. 81

"up into the pogo sky with arms akimbo," from "The Part Unseen," uncollected

"*His* light, his *light*, from off his face," from "Song," uncollected

Robert Duncan: "The Natural Doctrine" in *The Opening of the Field*, Grove Press, 1960, p. 81

William Carlos Williams: "Tree and Sky" in *The Collected Earlier Poems*, New Directions, 1951, p. 102

"Sky panels move and shift," from "The Dance That We Made" in *King of Shadows*, p. 159

"Once I was a sailor when the sky was one thing," from
"Shiver," uncollected

"Look at the sky: it reeks of projection," from "Still Walking,"
uncollected

"and edge to edge the blue absolute...," from "He Stood,"
uncollected

## SIX SKY POEMS

"The Place" and "In the Mist" are reprinted from *Into Distances*,
Sun & Moon Press, 1993.

*Into Distances* is now available as a .pdf download from Green
Integer at: http://www.greeninteger.com/book-digital.
cfm?-aaron-shurin-into-distances-&BookID=381

"The Part Unseen," "Song," "He Stood," and "Still Walking" are
uncollected.

## THE SKY IN *CITIZEN*

All quotations come from *Citizen*, City Lights Books, 2012.

## IMAGES

p. 12  The author as Puck, 1965

p. 32  Figure from Monte Albán

p. 57  Forget-me-nots from journal

## ACKNOWLEDGMENTS

Grateful acknowledgement is given to the people and presses who supported this work in its various parts: To Sharon O'Dair and Joseph Campagna who invited me to the Alabama symposium, and Jeanne Heuving who brought me into the UW Convergence. To the publications that have presented this specific work and its field of citations in periodical, online, or book form: *The Berkeley Poetry Review*, The Academy of American Poets at Poets.org, Gay Sunshine Press, Sun & Moon Press, Omnidawn, City Lights Books and the University of Michigan Press. And to the various friends and readers who listened to and attended this developing work as if I were giving them what they were giving me — generous and intimate care in the form of benevolent scrutiny — and who shared with me without blinking the tensions and wonders of surrendering to the art.

—A.S.

## AUDIO

To download a recording of Aaron Shurin reading from this book, please visit our website, www.entreriosbooks.com/audio. Select this title and enter the password:

**OBERON**

Recorded at Outpost Studios, San Francisco
April 12, 2017

*Thank you to recording engineer Jim Lively.*